PRAISE FOR SOPHOMORE SLUMP

"Leigh Chadwick's prose poems are shockingly blunt and compulsively tender. They are dangerous confessions shot out of the cannon of her restless imagination and aimed straight at your heart. Don't blink."

—Steve Almond, author of *All the Secrets of the World*

"Hanging out with Leigh Chadwick's poetry collection *Sophomore Slump* is like bumping into a friend you haven't seen in a decade, and picking up exactly where you left off. Maybe you and this friend have both listened to 'Debaser' by the Pixies for six weeks straight. Perhaps your 'dreams are nothing but a wall of owls,' or you have stumbled upon 'a sundress lumped in dust and asphalt, alone in the middle of Grand River Avenue.' Just when you think Chadwick's poems have reached the peak in their crescendo, they keep climbing. Chadwick grabs the most dazzling grotesque tableaus of the subconscious, then recasts them in the spirit of a music video worthy of a premium spot on *120 Minutes*."

—Mary Biddinger, author of *Department of Elegy*

"Leigh Chadwick's *Sophomore Slump* is a seriously hilarious romp, via prose poems. Chadwick uses the literary device of a lead singer in a band, complete with hits, demos, and bonus tracks, to wrap her mind around the folly of celebrity at a time of Earth's violence and peril, i.e. *How many forest fires would it take to melt all the baby Jesuses in the world?* She is not afraid to meet our cultural moment head on with all the urgency it requires. Chadwick is constantly assessing, sometimes farcically so—in 'Yelp Reviews of Past Loves'—and sometimes chillingly so—in 'A Comprehensive List of Places to Hide from a Bullet.' I couldn't help think of Harold Bloom's *Anxiety of Influence*—though Chadwick kicks Bloom and Freud to the curb. Her anxiety is not struggling to top her literary idols but instead hopes to top herself (which, of course, she does!)."

—Denise Duhamel, author of *Second Story*

"*Sophomore Slump* is a kaleidoscopic, versatile, and transgressive work of art. These poems—no, these glimpses into the heart—are full of irreverence and the practicality life needs to sustain itself. Unassumingly brilliant and funny, *Sophomore Slump* is an indelible work from an unforgettable writer."

—Morgan Talty, author of *Night of the Living Rez*

"Leigh Chadwick is the rockstar of poets, who are already the rockstars of writers, who are otherwise pretty dull people. *Sophomore Slump* is a certified banger."

—Mike Nagel, author of *Duplex*

PRAISE FOR LEIGH CHADWICK

"Leigh Chadwick is an absurdist with a heart of gold, funny and strange on the page and always precisely herself, no matter the persona she's taking on—including that of *Your Favorite Poet*. These poems are a party come to break your heart, wondrously smart and wonderfully weird."

—Matt Bell, author of *Appleseed*

"If Chadwick isn't your favorite poet, she may be your favorite poem."

—Alina Stefanescu, author of *Dor*

"Leigh Chadwick is the kind of poet who coats deep wounds with a miraculous salve . . . the kind of poet who knows the right questions to ask Jesus . . . the kind of poet who has written a flawless collection blending absurdity and luminosity."

—*Bending Genres*

"*Your Favorite Poet* is charming as hell."

—Amorak Huey,
author of *Dad Jokes from Late in the Patriarchy*

"Leigh Chadwick is reminiscent of Vonnegut in her ability to tell you what's wrong, what's bad, without standing on a soap box. Her poetry and her message are both immediate and impactful. She is one of the most authentic and exciting poets I've read."

—Travis Cravey, author of *Manifold*

"Chadwick has her finger squarely on the pulse of the contemporary moment, and her poems are funny, joyous, and sad. In short, they are a wonder."

—Andrew Bertaina,
author of *One Person Away From You*

"Somehow I get the feeling that since Leigh Chadwick is here to write about our world that everything will be all right."

—Maureen Seaton, author of *Undersea*

"To the very end pushing us past the expected boundaries of a poetry collection's architecture . . . Chadwick the poet casts a wistful spell toward the reader, that they might wish to read more words penned by this fantasticated bard. This reader would like to."

—*fck your bookclub*

"Leigh Chadwick is a master of building and deconstructing a scene, a writer so dexterous at pivoting from one image to the next and so wrecking-ball powerful at shattering a narrative that every poem left me steeped in delight or devastation, wondering: *how did she do that?*"

—Todd Dillard, author of *Ways We Vanish*

"Clear-eyed, open-hearted, defiantly gorgeous, and harrowing. Sign me up for everything else Leigh Chadwick ever writes."

—Ben Loory, author of *Tales of Falling and Flying*

ALSO BY LEIGH CHADWICK

Dating Pete Davidson

Too Much Tongue (co-written with Adrienne Marie Barrios)

Your Favorite Poet

This Is How We Learn to Pray (a poetry coloring book, illustrated Stephanie Kirsten)

Daughters of the State

SOPHOMORE SLUMP

LEIGH CHADWICK

Sophomore Slump ©2023 Leigh Chadwick.

All rights belong to the author.
Fair use quotes are welcome.

The cover was designed by Angelo Maneage.

The book was published by Malarkey Books. Their website is malarkeybooks.com.

The ISBN is 9798987465493.

For Adrienne Marie Barrios

PREFACE

The last book was better.

TABLE OF CONTENTS

STUDIO ALBUM

YOUR FAVORITE POET	29
LEAD SINGER OF THE BAND	30
J.LO DRESSES UP AS THE INTERNET WHILE I AM GIVEN A GRAMMY FOR WALKING IN A STRAIGHT LINE	31
AFTER LISTENING TO DEBASER BY THE PIXIES FOR A WEEK STRAIGHT	32
SOUTH FLORIDA	33
DECADES	34
I HAVE NOTHING IN MY HEART BUT MY HEART	35
SPRING POEM	36
EVERY HOLIDAY IS SOLD SEPARATELY	37
HOW TO GET OVER IT	38

"GLENDORA" IS MY SEVENTH-FAVORITE RILO KILEY SONG	39
MANIFEST DESTINY	40
I QUIT SMOKING BECAUSE I WAS TOLD I SHOULD QUIT SMOKING	42
I WONDER IF YOU WILL ALWAYS BE GOOD AT BEING MY HUSBAND	43
A ROOM FULL OF PICTURES OF MYSELF STARING AT PICTURES OF MYSELF (LIFE AT PARKWEST HOSPITAL; NOVEMBER 2020)	44
LEIGH CHADWICK	45
AFTER CHARACTER ACTRESS MARGOT MARTINDALE COMES HOME FROM WAR, SHE MAKES A CAMEO IN LEIGH CHADWICK'S POETRY COLLECTION *SOPHOMORE SLUMP*	46
HALLOWEEN POEM WRITTEN IN AUGUST	47
I WANT DORIS BURKE TO NARRATE MY LIFE	48
I VOTE JIMMY BUTLER'S CHEEKBONES THE POET LAUREATE OF MY DUVET	49

A LIST OF WHAT I'LL NEVER MISS	50
STEVEN, WHO LISTENED TO TOO MUCH BRIGHT EYES	51
A NOTE FROM THE AUTHOR	52

DEMOS

DEMO #1 (THE REDACTED SESSIONS)	55
DEMO #2 (THE REDACTED SESSIONS)	56
DEMO #3 (THE REDACTED SESSIONS)	57
DEMO #4 (THE REDACTED SESSIONS)	58
DEMO #5 (THE REDACTED SESSIONS)	59
DEMO #6 (THE REDACTED SESSIONS)	60
DEMO #7 (THE REDACTED SESSIONS)	61
DEMO #8 (THE REDACTED SESSIONS)	62

THE YELP REVIEWS OF PAST LOVES EP

YELP REVIEWS OF PAST LOVES	65
YELP REVIEWS OF PAST LOVES	66
YELP REVIEWS OF PAST LOVES	67

B-SIDES

A METAPHOR	71
YELLOW	72
DARIA FROM THE TV SHOW *DARIA*	73
THE FIRST POET TO FUCK ON THE MOON WILL OFFICIALLY WIN POETRY	77
UNTITLED	78
I WROTE THIS POEM WHILE LISTENING TO BELLE AND SEBASTIAN'S "IT COULD HAVE BEEN A BRILLIANT CAREER"	79

POEM WRITTEN WITH THE SOLE PURPOSE OF TRYING TO MAKE YOU NOSTALGIC ABOUT MY LAST POETRY COLLECTION, *YOUR FAVORITE POET*, ALSO PUBLISHED BY MALARKEY BOOKS, WHICH IS A BETTER BOOK THAN THIS ONE, THE ONE THAT YOU'RE CURRENTLY READING, SO IF YOU HAVEN'T PURCHASED A COPY OF *YOUR FAVORITE POET* YET, WHICH WAS ALSO PUBLISHED BY MALARKEY BOOKS, THEN YOU SHOULD DEFINITELY BUY IT NOW, LIKE RIGHT THIS SECOND, LIKE STOP READING THIS STUPIDLY LONG TITLE FOR A POEM AND GO BUY IT, AND IF YOU'RE WONDERING WHERE YOU CAN FIND A COPY OF *YOUR FAVORITE POET*, PUBLISHED BY MALARKEY BOOKS, YOU CAN GET IT DIRECTLY FROM THE PUBLISHER'S WEBSITE, OR THROUGH AMAZON.COM OR BOOKSHOP.ORG OR IN PERSON AT POWELL'S, WHICH IS LOCATED IN PORTLAND, OREGON, NOT PORTLAND, MAINE, IN CASE YOU WERE CONFUSED, OR IF IT'S STILL IN STOCK, YOU CAN WALK INTO RAVEN BOOK STORE, WHICH IS LOCATED IN LAWRENCE, KANSAS, AND PICK UP A COPY, BUT ANYWAY, NOW YOU KNOW THERE ARE A LOT OF PLACES YOU CAN BUY *YOUR FAVORITE POET*, WHICH WAS PUBLISHED BY MALARKEY BOOKS, A BOOK THAT IS BETTER THAN THIS ONE

POEM ABOUT *FRIDAY NIGHT LIGHTS*, KYRIE IRVING, AND AARON RODGERS THAT ALSO REFERENCES THE FLAMING LIPS	82
AN EXCERPT FROM TAYLOR SWIFT'S DIARY ENTRY WRITTEN SEVEN MONTHS AFTER BREAKING UP WITH TAYLOR LAUTNER	84
AN ESSAY ABOUT TIME TRAVEL	85
THE ONE WHERE ERIC AND DYLAN WALK INTO A LIBRARY	86
MONSTER MONSTER MONSTER	87
A LIST OF SYNONYMS FOR THE WORD *GHOST*	93
A LIST OF WHAT I FOUND IN THE RESTROOM OF THE TACO BELL OFF KINGSTON BOULEVARD	94
MY DAUGHTER KEEPS DROPPING FOOD ON THE FLOOR AND NOW THE DOG IS BECOMING OBESE	95

I THOUGHT ABOUT THE FILM *GOOD WILL HUNTING*—DIRECTED BY OSCAR-NOMINEE GUS VAN SANT (*DRUGSTORE COWBOY, MILK, ELEPHANT*), AND STARRING OSCAR-WINNER MATT DAMON (*THE BOURNE IDENTITY, THE BOURNE SUPREMACY, WE BOUGHT A ZOO*) AS MATH PRODIGY WILL HUNTING, AND OSCAR-WINNER BEN AFFLECK (*GIGLI, MALLRATS, REINDEER GAMES*) AS MATH PRODIGY WILL HUNTING'S BEST FRIEND, AND OSCAR-NOMINEE MINNIE DRIVER (*RETURN TO ME, RETURN TO ZERO, HOPE SPRINGS*) AS MATH PRODIGY WILL HUNTING'S LOVE INTEREST, AND OSCAR-WINNER ROBIN WILLIAMS (*DEAD POETS SOCIETY, MRS. DOUBTFIRE, JUMANJI*) AS MATH PRODIGY WILL HUNTING'S PSYCHOLOGIST WHO HAS A PENCHANT FOR BEARDS AND BOOKS AND CAN'T GET OVER THE WAY HIS DEAD WIFE USED TO FART IN HER SLEEP—APPROXIMATELY FOUR TIMES WHILE WRITING THIS POEM   96

I TAKE A ROCKET INTO SPACE
AND FORGET WHY I WENT INTO SPACE   98

A COMPREHENSIVE LIST
OF PLACES TO HIDE FROM A BULLET   99

SETLIST FOR LEIGH CHADWICK'S NORTH AMERICAN TOUR

HOW DO I TELL MY DAUGHTER WHEN SHE IS OLD ENOUGH FOR ME TO TELL HER	109
HOW MANY TIMES IS TOO MANY TIMES TO LISTEN TO REGINA SPEKTOR'S "US" ON REPEAT?	110
I WAS STILL LISTENING TO BELLE AND SEBASTIAN'S "IT COULD HAVE BEEN A BRILLIANT CAREER" WHEN I WROTE THIS POEM	111
I CALL YOU MY HUSBAND	113
I WANT TO LIVE SOFTLY	114
EVERY DAY IS A GOOD DAY TO LISTEN TO "SOMEDAY" (REMASTERED)	115
IT'S TRUE	117
AN EMPTY CLOSET IS STILL A CLOSET	118
UNCORRECTED PROOF	119

ANYTHING CAN HAPPEN IN A PARK
IF YOU CALL EVERYTHING A PARK   121

I WANTED TO NAME MY DAUGHTER PRIMROSE BUT EVERYONE SAID NO, LEIGH, THAT'S DUMB, SO I DIDN'T NAME MY DAUGHTER PRIMROSE, BUT NO ONE CAN TELL ME WHAT I CAN OR CAN'T TITLE MY POEMS, SO FUCK IT, THIS POEM IS TITLED "PRIMROSE"   122

DELETED SCENES FROM THE MUSIC VIDEO
FOR CAKE'S 2001 HIT SONG
"SHORT SKIRT / LONG JACKET"   123

MVP   124

WHILE ON THE VERGE OF WANTING
TO JUMP OFF A CLIFF, I WRITE A POEM   125

WHAT COMMAS   126

NOVEMBER IS A MONTH I GUESS   127

DUETS

WHAT COMES NEXT
(Co-written with Adrienne Marie Barrios)   131

THERE IS NO ANSWER TO THE SIMPLICITY
OF WEATHER
(Co-written with Mitchell Nobis)   133

WHAT SWALLOWS BUT DOESN'T SEE
(Co-written with Mitchell Nobis)   134

I LIKE TO THINK PROPER FIRST THING
IN THE MORNING
(Co-written with Andrew Bertaina)   136

PLEASE MIX AND MESH AND MOLD AND FOLD
(Co-written with Ben Niespodziany)   137

DAY TO DAY
(Co-written with Mitchell Nobis)   138

HOSPITAL GOWN
(Co-written with Ben Niespodziany)   139

THAT'S STILL SHORT TERM.
I CARE ABOUT LONG TERM.
(Co-written with Adrienne Marie Barrios)   140

HIT SINGLES

GREG ABBOTT CAN GO FUCK HIMSELF	143
APRIL IS ITS OWN WEATHER	145
IF THE TRUTH IS OUT THERE, I QUIT	146
ANXIOUS LOVE	148
THE GREEN FERN	149
A POEM NOT ABOUT BEARS	150
(INTERLUDE)	151

I GOT DEPRESSED SO I DECIDED TO WRITE A BOOK ABOUT BEING DEPRESSED, AND IT'S ACTUALLY THIS BOOK, *SOPHOMORE SLUMP*, THE ONE YOU'RE HOLDING IN YOUR HANDS (AND GOODNESS WHAT LOVELY HANDS THEY ARE), THE ONE YOU ARE JUST ABOUT FINISHED READING, AND BY THE WAY, WHILE YOU'RE HERE, LET ME JUST SAY THANK YOU FOR READING IT, THIS LITTLE, SAD BOOK I WROTE AND TITLED *SOPHOMORE SLUMP*, AND HOPEFULLY YOU BOUGHT THIS COPY YOU'RE READING BECAUSE HOLY SHIT DAYCARE IS EXPENSIVE, BUT EVEN IF YOU DIDN'T BUY IT

AND INSTEAD, YOU SHOPLIFTED IT FROM AN INDEPENDENT BOOKSTORE (PRETTY SHITTY OF YOU, TO BE HONEST) OR READ IT HUNCHED IN THE CORNER OF YOUR LOCAL LIBRARY (THAT WOULD BE OKAY!) OR ORDERED IT OFF AMAZON AND THEN RETURNED IT (STILL PRETTY SHITTY BUT HEY, WHATEVER) OR STOLE IT FROM AN EX-LOVER (ALSO A TOTALLY OKAY THING TO DO!), I AM STILL GLAD YOU ARE HERE (EMO IN C MINOR)   152

THANK YOU

ACKNOWLEDGMENTS

ABOUT THE AUTHOR

DELUXE EDITION WITH BONUS TRACKS

FOREVER   161

STILL YOUR FAVORITE POET   163

STUDIO ALBUM

YOUR FAVORITE POET

For foreplay, I don't have sex with our marriage counselor. Still, the pineapple in the fridge is ripe, and I came four times this morning. After, I took a nap and dreamed in assembly lines. When I woke up, I was dressed in left turns. Outside, the woods are gaining weight. The trees are starting to look like trees, again. I haven't checked the mail in weeks, so I go out to the mailbox. It's filled with frequent flier miles and an RSVP from our neighbor inviting us to come watch him mow his lawn. You're still getting nosebleeds. You tell me not to worry, but I worry. I think it's spring, but I never took calculus in high school so it's impossible to tell. In the guest bedroom, I can hear Sisyphus yawn. You tell me it'd be nice to find some air, so I pour us each a glass of grapes and we go out into the backyard. The sky is dim, like the lowest setting on a lamp. It's clear enough that you can look up and not get lost in thought bubbles. I point to the brightest thing above us. *Do you think that's the moon or a hangnail?* I ask. I'm not sure. I never am. Below the moon or the hangnail, the grass grazes my ankles. It makes me think of antlers, but I don't know why.

LEAD SINGER OF THE BAND

I am the lead singer of the band. I am not a good lead singer. We are not a good band. My voice is powder. My voice is thirty seconds into a cough drop. My voice faucets. I am the lead singer of the band. I do it for the ass. The bathroom stalls of dicks. The free drinks and unplugged smoke alarms. I am the lead singer of the band who goes on stage and makes balloon animals. Here's a giraffe. Here's an elephant that lost its tusks. Just kidding—that shit was sawed off. I am the lead singer of the band. I chain smoke in alleys, pull my skirt up while my bassist presses my back against the green dumpster. I always keep the cigarette lit. I am the lead singer of the band that tours the country in a van, playing gigs to Christmas ornaments and wayward hearts and lost and broken children. I am the lead singer of the band that you have never heard of but have dreamed about, this sound we make: the buzz of an amp, the out-of-tune Fender, the *tap tap tap* of the hi-hat. I am the lead singer of the band with a tambourine player. His name is Steve. He is allergic to bees. We are all allergic to bees.

J.LO DRESSES UP AS THE INTERNET WHILE I AM GIVEN A GRAMMY FOR WALKING IN A STRAIGHT LINE

I masturbate to the rhythm of the drum fill on "In the Air Tonight." After, I go to the bathroom and piss sunflowers. I am given a Grammy for pissing sunflowers. I flush the toilet and wash my hands. When I get out of the bathroom, I am given a Grammy for washing my hands for a full twenty seconds. By the time I'm down the hall and heading into the kitchen, I am given a Grammy for being given a Grammy. I eat a bowl of Lucky Charms, but I don't win shit. I make a grocery list and am given a Grammy for never winning a Pulitzer. I call you on your way home from work and invite you over even though you already live here. For dinner, I feed you the right shoulder of Lady Gaga's dress made of sirloin. For foreplay, I dress up as Björk dressing up as a swan. I tattoo *show me you got prettier* on the inside of my right thigh. I invite your mouth to my left thigh and the bruises that haven't been bruised yet. By last call, I am given a Grammy for sweating from the hips, for sweating from the thighs, for sweating from every part of your lips that touch the parts of mine.

AFTER LISTENING TO DEBASER BY THE PIXIES FOR A WEEK STRAIGHT

I wake up with a hole in my leg. I wake up three toes too long. I birth myself birthing myself. Shit is gross. I wake up full of facts: going to the post office causes cancer, waking up causes cancer, light beer causes cancer, reunion tours cause cancer, cancer causes cancer. I wake up and everything feels like a griddle. My heart on a fryer. My head in the dryer. Even the moon is a heater. Who'd've thunk I'd get tired of never going bowling? Or watching eyes watching other eyes? Or grooving from the hips? I wake up because sometimes all it takes is a knife. A film strip through threaded fingers. The thought of *sometimes* as a billionaire explodes in space.

SOUTH FLORIDA

The morning rises every morning. I dream my head bleeding. I don't know why. When I wake up, I dress my eyes in Gucci and coat my throat in Motrin. For breakfast, I fall in love with your nose three times. Outside, willows weep. Jesus keeps sneezing from all the myrrh. Days dressed as toothpaste, I tell you I wish I had a reason to walk you home from school. It's a light beer kind of day. On TV, Jimmy Butler walks up and down the aisle of a private jet, singing Hootie & the Blowfish. For lunch, I subtweet my subtweets. I take you to the zoo where we spend the afternoon staring at the sky, counting the balloons vacationing in the clouds. I wear you home even though you're a decade too heavy. For dinner, I build you a poem about the river that swallowed the smaller river. I tell you, *Eventually, even water goes dry*. I tell you, *I could kiss you and I know exactly why*.

DECADES

Bad sex begets anxiety begets ulcers begets the only thing left growing is fingernails. It's easy to forget the weather whenever you make it to last call. In twenty years, I still will never have dreamt in French. In twenty years, I will be twenty years older. In twenty years, if you look hard enough, you will see everything we have chosen to forget: newlyweds glamping in a yurt, planting mistletoes in the Pottery Barn in the West Town Mall, fingernails growing through dirt, teaching my daughter how to floss while a river swallows a schoolyard, the fire in the forest built after the last fire that burned down the forest, and me standing in the middle of an empty cornfield—nothing more than a scribbled-out acronym.

I HAVE NOTHING IN MY HEART BUT MY HEART

One is enough, God says, pointing at my heart. I nod to my feelings, thick as mud. I watch what blooms stop blooming. I tell the monster under my bed that I am sick in the worst way. The monster doesn't say anything because the monster doesn't speak prose poem. I look at the freckles on my wrist. The freckles are shaped like freckles. I was going to mention the stork that left my daughter on our doorstep two Novembers ago, but I got a letter in the mail informing me that the birds are threatening to sue the poets for defamation. If I'm not listening to Modest Mouse, then I'm not listening to Modest Mouse, but most of the time I'm listening to Modest Mouse. My favorite hobby is getting off on the mundane, so for foreplay, I watch you take out the trash, flush the dead goldfish down the toilet. My favorite orgasm is watching basketball while you build an amusement park between my thighs. People won't stop dying, and I'm not sure what else there is to say about that except that people won't stop dying. I don't know what to do. There are so many bombs and bullets, and the sequel to *Contagion* is longer than *Titanic*. Anyway, Sisyphus finally got that goddamn boulder up that goddamn hill. He's at home now, on the phone, setting up an appointment with his chiropractor.

SPRING POEM

I'm watching the days bleed into spring. I don't know why I used the word *bleed*; I hate it, the word. Makes me think of school halls and schoolyards, a teacher as shield, a student as target practice, an entire classroom smoking pipe bombs as a Surgeon General's Warning on the back of my eyelids reads *Smoking pipe bombs will lead to loss of limbs and most likely death*. There was a time I used to be happy. This was before I lost my heart somewhere south of the Mason-Dixon line. I've ordered a new heart, but it's currently on backorder. It's a supply chain issue, I'm told. The trees are becoming trees again. My daughter can now open doors. It's frightening how fast a weed can grow, how quickly a lung can cave, how quietly we find ourselves escaping.

EVERY HOLIDAY IS SOLD SEPARATELY

The day before Christmas Eve is when I tattoo *HUG LIFE* across my abdomen. Lately I've been dreaming landlocked. My favorite instrument is the Bermuda Triangle. My favorite family is the one I'll still have tomorrow. I never think about winter until after it's gone. Christmas is a strange time to stare into people's yards: plastic babies swaddled in plastic blankets resting in plastic hay. Rainbows melting off roofs. Mariah Carey going door to door, caroling to you, for you, about you. Christmas is Halloween born again, when everywhere Jesus dresses up like a baby and takes a nap in your yard. I ask Siri, *How many forest fires would it take to melt all the baby Jesuses in the world?* Siri says, *Seven. The answer is always seven.*

HOW TO GET OVER IT

Call your psychiatrist. Tell him to put more Xanax in your Xanax. Drink everything straight from the bottle. Dream Eve napping in a pit of snakes. Bathe in the Mississippi. Listen to Elliott Smith with your eyes closed, an unlit cigarette cradled behind your left ear. Call God collect. Make him apologize for not doing better. Tattoo *you will never be prettier* on the inside of your eyelids. Wonder if body bags ever commit suicide. Tell your psychiatrist to refill the Xanax he put in your Xanax. Find your husband exactly where he said he would be. Feel slightly disappointed. Teach yourself how to read so you can order off the takeout menu at Chili's. Remember you hate Chili's. Regret learning how to read. Pretend stoplights are bad at their jobs. Pretend that one day you will rewrite this poem and that it will start something like *Poetry is the well I dip my head into when my mouth goes cotton*. Pretend you will one day find the beige cardigan you left in an Uber sometime last winter. Pretend you never opened the garage door. Pretend you are done pretending.

"GLENDORA" IS MY SEVENTH-FAVORITE RILO KILEY SONG

I miss the days I used to count sheep dressed as sheep, days I flossed with boneyards and got sick off vodka and cranberry or vodka and orange juice or sometimes just vodka while blossoms bloomed and I would grow flushed with lust. Days I fell asleep in a bed in Nashville and dreamt a sandstorm in the Coliseum as I stood at the edge of the arena, my sword pressed through skin as plastic buckets were filled with what plastic buckets should never be filled.

MANIFEST DESTINY

The police chief referred to it as a *really tragic situation*. Well, no shit. Six dead, at least ten injured. Another gun, another city. I was about to eat a madeleine dipped in chocolate when I heard the news, but now I've lost my appetite, and I just want to throw the cookie in the trash, tie my daughter to my back, and just go, just run—to where, it doesn't matter, because who knows where's next. Who knows who's next. Who knows where the who is next. See, guns are everywhere. So are cities. So are restaurants and bars and nightclubs and concerts and supermarkets and schools. This time it was Sacramento. Not counting this time but also counting this time, it was also Dallas, but that's another poem. I'm sorry, I don't have the energy for two of these, so here is where I tell you to open an atlas and press the tip of your index finger on the map and say, *Look, there is a gun learning how to be a gun. Do you see it?* Six dressed in body bags and another ten in hospital gowns. This time it wasn't Austin or Boulder or Atlanta or Las Vegas or Orlando or that other city in Florida. It was Sacramento, not far from the Golden 1 Center, where the Kings continue to lose games, where they go another season without making the playoffs, where someone could hope for the ball to hit nothing but net instead of a bullet hitting nothing but organ.

I QUIT SMOKING BECAUSE I WAS TOLD I SHOULD QUIT SMOKING

I used to listen to Iron & Wine to help myself fall asleep. Now, I walk through walls and crisscross the sun until I'm too tired to stand. Somewhere and everywhere, a baby cries. I miss the last Camel Light in the pack of Camel Lights. Flipped upside down. Lighting cherry. Waiting for the luck that will never come.

I WONDER IF YOU WILL ALWAYS BE GOOD AT BEING MY HUSBAND

Walking home from the bar down streets still covered in decades-old dust—something cancerous and stained—we each buy a slice of pizza and only eat the crust. We keep walking and my mind wanders, slips, grows a wither, and then I'm wondering if you will always be good at being my husband, and then I'm thinking about animal husbandry, and why is animal husbandry called animal husbandry, I don't know, and I'm wondering who I could ask why animal husbandry is called animal husbandry but I don't know anyone to ask, and then I'm wondering when was the last time I smelled something mellifluous and who in this moment is hiding behind a slab of Kevlar or ducking in a bomb shelter and how big is an ostrich heart and who will never need an alarm clock ever again?

A ROOM FULL OF PICTURES OF ME STARING AT PICTURES OF MYSELF (LIVE AT PARKWEST HOSPITAL, NOVEMBER 2020)

I go into a room and come out a mother. I birth a second mother. The second mother is hungry, so I spend my afternoons finding low-income housing for my feelings: The feeling of running toward a gun. The feeling of running from a gun. The feeling of waking up in the middle of a disaster movie, lost in a closeup, hips sweating from bruised lips. The feeling of a gun, any gun, pointing at someone, anyone, someone's anyone.

LEIGH CHADWICK

I fall asleep on the couch covered in brushed sheep. If my dreams went viral, I'd probably be arrested. When I wake up, I'm in a recording studio, my mouth inches from a microphone. I'm holding a guitar plugged into an amp. The guitar is shaped like a pharmacy. I strum the guitar and a handful of Adderall spills out of the amp. I swallow two pills and tell the microphone, *I miss the youth of my youth.* I feel alive in the worst way. I am awake, wide, thighs pressed together, broken nails and red knees. I tell the microphone, *I want to kiss everything that was never given a chance to blossom.* I take another pill and wonder what yesterday is doing right now. I wonder what it must be like to whisper a horse awake. I strum the guitar again and a bottle of Xanax rolls across the room. Someone puts a cigarette behind my ear as I tell the microphone, *It's the monotony of roller coasters that scares me the most.*

AFTER CHARACTER ACTRESS MARGOT MARTINDALE COMES HOME FROM WAR, SHE MAKES A CAMEO IN LEIGH CHADWICK'S POETRY COLLECTION SOPHOMORE SLUMP

Call me horse heart, Margot Martindale tells me. She has just come back from war. I ask her who won, but she doesn't know. She's unsure if it matters. Instead, she shows me her feathered helmet rusted from blood and how it's caked in everything left in the kitchen pantry: the hole in the ozone layer, drunk texts, frequent flier miles, birthmarks over hip bones. Outside is nothing but rain and clouds yelling at each other, slamming their bedroom doors, canceling future therapy appointments. The rain makes me think of a city sinking, and then I'm looking at my hands, how they have nowhere to go. I put on a pot of tea while Margot Martindale puts on a pair of rain boots and goes out into the yard. She tries to jump in the puddles, but she just floats above them, the raindrops falling through her. The teapot whistles. Margot Martindale is still floating as the clouds stop coughing, as I pour the boiling water into a mug.

HALLOWEEN POEM WRITTEN IN AUGUST

For Halloween, I save an abandoned monster from crossing a crowded interstate. I take the monster home. I ask the monster if it's hungry and the monster nods, so I heat up some leftover meatloaf I made last Thursday. The monster eats the meatloaf while I go into the bathroom and shave my legs, even though I know I won't see you for another week, once you finally get back from your trip overseas, where you're volunteering with Pumpkin Carving Without Borders. *What a ghoul*, your last postcard you mailed to me said, *to leave your skin dressed without touch*. I wrote back, *I miss having your toothbrush next to mine and yelling at you for leaving tiny hairs in the sink after you shave*. After giving out bite-size Snickers and Three Musketeers and Milky Way bars to children dressed as lazy ghosts, radioactive turtles, scarecrows that have run away from the cornfields of Iowa, Taylor Swift's favorite cardigan, and Rupi Kaur's bank account, the monster and I share a bag of microwaved popcorn and watch a movie on Netflix. In the movie, a character named after a city in the Midwest says, *Feminists are more likely to do anal*. I don't know if that's true. I ask you if you think that's true before remembering that, even though I shaved my legs, you're still not here.

I WANT DORIS BURKE TO NARRATE MY LIFE

I had a baby because of basketball. Don't ask. Studies show it is easier to hate-fuck than to cry. Studies show if you step on a Woj Bomb, you will end up trapped in Oklahoma, hoping for lightning to follow the cracks in your jersey. In the beginning, God put rockets on Vince Carter's feet and made milk cartons because he knew basketball players would end up going missing. Which reminds me: Who stole Roy Hibbert, and why didn't they do it sooner? And is J.R. Smith still naked from the waist up? And does Melo use fabric softener while running his hoodie through the wash? And does Seattle miss going hedgehog? And why was Anthony Davis's body born a mockingbird? I still have so many questions, but I don't have the time to list them here—I'm too busy burying Dwyane Wade's talking cube in a pocket of earth, between *Grantland* and Linsanity, while teaching Alex Caruso how to build an Etsy page so he has somewhere to sell the headbands he sews during offseason.

I VOTE JIMMY BUTLER'S CHEEKBONES THE POET LAUREATE OF MY DUVET

Jimmy Butler plays Jimmy Buckets in a movie about Jimmy Buckets draining dreams off the cliff of a pier in South Beach, *Sleepless in Miami*, based on a true story, inspired by the sharpness of welded cheekbones pressed pillow-deep, scissors next to a faceless picture of last year's MVP, cans of Milwaukee's Best littering the parking lot of what used to be the American Airlines Arena. Now it's the FTX Arena. Nothing stays. Still, I like the nights when you touch the places I want you to touch, and then the mornings after: the hot water from the showerhead, the lip I used to never chew, the TV turned to ESPN, sound muted, clips of buckets traded for other buckets, an arena of signed hardcovers dressed as a Camel Light, as the heat of the midmorning drips over the limp lip of Miami.

A LIST OF WHAT I'LL NEVER MISS

I grow mistletoes in the attic of hell. I jump off a bridge so I can say I jumped off a bridge. It doesn't go well. Hobbled from the heart down, I make a list of what I'll never miss: the days before I was called mother; thoughts about quicksand; fucking my third boyfriend, Mark, in the back of his mother's Explorer parked behind the Bank of America off Kingston Boulevard, the seatbelt digging into my ass, a lack of moisture between my thighs. It's always a Tuesday when I wake up lonely in a lonely way. For therapy, I order a quarter pounder with cheese. I'm not tired, I'm fucking exhausted. Still. The days tick toward a decade, and I still find my lipstick smeared, sweat slick as grease, my body prostrate as you slide me through the blush of a Sunday afternoon.

STEVEN, WHO LISTENED TO TOO MUCH BRIGHT EYES

It's the Valium dripping down my throat that blurs the weather. What doesn't crash will soon. It's the reverb of Omaha that gives the Midwest a migraine. I hear he owns a bar now. I hear he called my old roommate, and that it took him three syllables to say *Leigh*.

A NOTE FROM THE AUTHOR

I'd carry you home, if only you'd fit.

DEMOS

DEMO #1 (FROM THE REDACTED SESSIONS)

[Redacted] never gets dehydrated from the hips down. [Redacted] thinks the new stuff is okay, but she prefers what came yesterday. He said she woke up smelling like a mausoleum. He said that when she cried, her tears were always off camera. He said it's sad—to only be there to fill a set, to help push a scene along.

DEMO #2 (FROM THE REDACTED SESSIONS)

[Redacted] understands the brilliance of sorrow. She dreams in cobwebs, of waking up in nets of silk. Her favorite dreams are when she dreams that she never dreams. She dreams her dreams are as empty as her stomach, as empty as the bottle of lotion on the nightstand, as empty as the bottle of bleach her mother poured over her sister two days before Thanksgiving.

DEMO #3 (FROM THE REDACTED SESSIONS)

[Redacted] tells him that her favorite word is *violet*. He is standing in front of her. He is redwood-stiff, built like a high rise. She imagines him the entire Sierra Nevada. They are in a bedroom or a Red Roof Inn. Or maybe it's a Super 8. Could be a Motel 6 or an apartment off I-95. [Redacted] can't remember. It doesn't matter. A bed is a bed is a bed is a bed, and she is sitting on the edge of one of those beds. Her hands are greasy. An empty package of McDonald's French fries is on the nightstand, next to a half-eaten quarter pounder with cheese. [Redacted] forgot to tell them to hold the pickles. Crumbs on the bedspread. The air conditioner clicks on, and with it a slight hum, the only sound in the room. There is dirt on her neck, between her breasts. *Did I put on lipstick?* she wonders. She watches him take off his shoes. Neither of them says anything. He unbuckles his belt, pulls down his jeans. He doesn't bother taking off his socks. Still. Everything is still, except for the slight hum from the air conditioner and his shadow as it scratches [Redacted]'s chin, then neck, followed by the shade of the world between her lips, pressed so gently against her tongue.

DEMO #4 (FROM THE REDACTED SESSIONS)

A crash quickly followed by a second. It comes from the apartment next door. The sound shakes [Redacted], and she jolts out of bed, knocking the ashtray off her stomach. The ashtray lands upside down on her comforter, scattering ash across the bed. The cigarette stays glued between her fingers. It's [Redacted]'s neighbors inventing manmade thunder. Again. [Redacted] settles back down on the bed and imagines someone in the apartment next to hers floating midair, arms outstretched, shooting bolts of lightning from their fingertips. She imagines a relationship ending or beginning, maybe someone being murdered and brought back to life for no other reason than so they could be murdered all over again. A third crash. The glass on [Redacted]'s nightstand topples over and breaks, water spilling rivulets through the tile cracks. The walls creak as something goes thump. [Redacted] imagines a disaster film—the San Andreas Fault cracking in half as families or parts of families fall through never-ending holes covered in shuttered darkness—as she picks up the ashtray off the comforter and dusts ash onto the floor. [Redacted] takes the last drag of her cigarette before dropping the butt into the ashtray, not bothering to stub it out.

DEMO #5 (FROM THE REDACTED SESSIONS)

[Redacted] was never taught how loud to scream, how loud to moan into a pillowcase covered in everything her face touched last month. [Redacted] hasn't washed herself in days. The longer she stays in bed, the quieter her name becomes.

DEMO #6 (FROM THE REDACTED SESSIONS)

And now [Redacted]'s here. It's familiar, this here. This blood. That twang. That eighty-pound heart. It's familiar. Those sunken temples. Those broken ribs. The field of rosebuds. The ash an ant pile on the linoleum floor. And then. She checks her palms. And then. Her eyes all sockets. And then. She wonders how she got here. She wonders where this goes. And then. The steering wheel turns. And then. Nothing but grass and beer bottles buried beneath the sprinklers. And then. Stupid poets howling at the moon. And then. [Redacted] dreams of rosebuds. She wakes up half tree.

DEMO #7 (THE REDACTED SESSIONS)

[Redacted] looks out the window. The sky is frowning. There's a brief flash; the windows shudder. [Redacted] counts the seconds between the lightning and the thunder and thinks, *What boldness, waiting for the tip of tomorrow.* She makes it to four seconds before another flash of light. It's the slow four seconds—counted in hushed Mississippis—where four seconds equals four miles. Someone taught [Redacted] this once, but she doesn't remember who. Maybe it was her mother, before she took that last hit and stopped being her mother. Rain begins to fall, then curls like the bottom of an umbrella, which makes [Redacted] think that everything is broken, and if it's not already broken then it should be, because she wonders, *What has a rose ever taught me about love?*

DEMO #8 (FROM THE REDACTED SESSIONS)

[Redacted] has scars on her cheeks because her father decided he wanted to put them there, and so parts of her face are tiny speedbumps. Twelve years after the scars, [Redacted]'s boyfriend shits blood for three days, but he doesn't know why. They share a needle in the back of a Greyhound that's headed to Memphis. [Redacted] wants to ask her boyfriend, *Are there any phone calls that are considered long distance anymore?* He doesn't answer the question. Instead, she watches a shadow walk across his chin. A week later, there will be no one left to say, *I didn't see the ditch coming.*

THE YELP REVIEWS OF PAST LOVES EP

YELP REVIEWS OF PAST LOVES

Leigh C.
Oak Ridge, TN
0 friends
3 reviews
0 photos

08/04/2020

Holly HIlls Summer Camp

Jason R. tasted like pencil shavings. We were both nine, though he was six weeks older. It was a thing. Summer camp in July. The sky smelled like cherries. There were monkey bars, but we weren't standing under them. Instead, they hung in the background like a city skyline. Jason told me to open my mouth and then he licked my front teeth. This was a week after a camp counselor had to cut a wad of bubblegum out of my hair. Inches. It was inches. A clump of blonde spiderwebs.

YELP REVIEWS OF PAST LOVES

Leigh C.
Oak Ridge, TN
0 friends
18 reviews
0 photos

Starbucks

10/07/2020

Will H. and I fucked once. It felt like a discounted massage. I met Will shortly after graduating from Delta State University—a small college in the middle of a Mississippi Delta sigh—with a BA in English and a teacher's certification I'd realize, years later, I never wanted. Will and I both worked at Starbucks, where we'd spend the lulls of our morning shifts sharing Parliaments while leaning against the green dumpster that flanked the south corner of a strip mall off Griffin Blvd. I was halfway through what I had planned to be my year of self-discovery, of learning how to move in slow motion, of dreaming in French and smoking cigarettes dipped in vanilla and packaged in metal tins. All of this to say I packed a suitcase and drove my '92 Corolla to my grandmother's condo in Boca Raton, where I slept in her guest bedroom and spent the evenings eating leftover stroganoff and watching *Jeopardy!* I was 22. I was waiting for my life to become something, anything: An art installation. A bottomless mimosa. A dresser drawer filled with lace.

YELP REVIEWS OF PAST LOVES

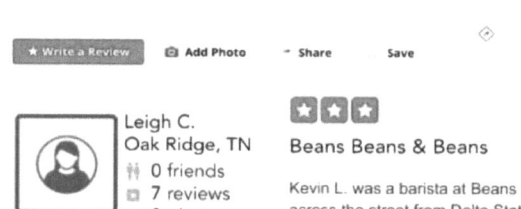

Leigh C.
Oak Ridge, TN
0 friends
7 reviews
0 photos

★★★ 11/06/2020

Beans Beans & Beans

Kevin L. was a barista at Beans Beans & Beans, a coffee shop across the street from Delta State University, where we both went to school. I was a sophomore,19, when he poured me a blonde roast. Kevin never put flowers in his beard but he only drank IPAs. He smoked marijuana cigarettes, built a compost in the backyard of the house he was subletting from a friend's friend. His shits smelled awful, but fucking him meant I went two months without having to pay for coffee. Plus, he touched carefully, and when he entered me, everything slowed. Kevin didn't own a car, but his bike cost two months' rent. His deodorant was natural, meaning it didn't work, so he always smelled slightly disposable, but I never came so hard as when his mouth reached between my thighs.

B-SIDES

A METAPHOR

He was in a band and then he was in another band and then there was the side project that was also a band and that other side project that was also a band and then he went solo because eventually everyone goes solo and then there was that other band before he went back to the first band.

YELLOW

Two years and seven minutes after our first fuck, we leave each other so we can say we left each other. *Everyone tries too hard at twenty-two.* Eight years later and sometimes my bones get so tired they run away and hide in cave drawings in the basements of museums. *If you're not crying, you should be.* What I mean is this morning I woke up at a birthday party and got lost in a field of summers. What I mean is every bird is yellow if yellow is the only color you can see.

DARIA FROM THE TV SHOW DARIA

One of the first girls I taught at The Agency looked like Daria from the TV show *Daria*, if Daria developed an eating disorder and occasionally hit her head against the wall.

Her name was Penelope and she smelled like toothpicks and gum disease. Inside or outside, in the middle of crowds or alone with a bathroom pass, she always walked in a straight line, one foot in front of the other, never side by side. It impressed me, the practice and effort it must've taken to live in such exacts. It seemed like she was attempting to find grace. I hoped she'd eventually find it.

Penelope was never not alone. She never had a visitor during weekly visitation, but that never stopped her from showing up and watching the side hugs or full hugs, the transference of pain from one of the girls to a grandmother or aunt. Occasionally, on those Wednesday afternoons, when it was my turn to supervise during visitation hours, I'd catch Penelope in a corner of the courtyard, next to a fake tree, perched on one leg like a flamingo.

Months would go by without an in-person visit from her DCS caseworker. Not that this was a surprise. There was never a point in learning any of the DCS staff's names—they rarely stayed in the job for more than a year, and often their stints were much shorter. I found myself surprised if one or two of them would scrape through a season. Doe-eyed, straight out of undergrad, middle class and ready to save the world, the majority of the DCS caseworkers just weren't cut out for it. They expected to be a walk-on on a TV show. Instead, they were starring in real life, with real pain and real actions that led to real consequences. I wish someone had warned them, said, *Hey, no, let's maybe not—have you considered teaching elementary school or writing grants for nonprofits?* Or, if someone did warn them and they still wanted to do it, that they'd try harder. I didn't blame them for leaving, but it didn't stop me from hating them. Each one was just one more adult who failed the girls. One more adult that abandoned them. One more adult that covered them in dust. Though Penelope never complained.

Through winter and then fall and into spring, Penelope's anorexia stiffened. She was at The Agency for no other reason than because of space, or lack of it, and maybe she thought if she let herself shrink, if she didn't need more room, then a home would open for her, and she'd just squeeze through the front door and share a house with people who wanted to pretend to try to be a family.

The psychologist at The Agency tried to bribe Penelope with powdered doughnuts, Yoo-hoo in the glass bottle, which tastes better than Yoo-hoo from the paper juice box, though it did little to persuade her. Penelope would take a bite of a doughnut and with powder on her lips, say thank you as she got up, leaving the Yoo-hoo on the desk, unopened.

Penelope was smart. She finished her courses and earned her high school diploma less than six months after arriving at The Agency. Because she was part of the foster system, Penelope was offered free tuition, along with room and board, to the local community college. She would also receive a small monthly stipend. When her new DCS caseworker told her, she said thank you the same way she did when handed a bottle of Yoo-hoo and then walked in a straight line to the bathroom and didn't come out for an hour.

One day, I asked Penelope what she wanted to do when she grew up. She looked at me like it was the dumbest thing anyone ever asked her, as if it were the dumbest thing anyone in the world had ever asked anyone.

I want to pet animals, she said.

Penelope spent eighteen months at The Agency, before turning eighteen and aging out of the system. I don't know what happens when the girls leave. I don't know if Penelope ever went to college. I don't know if she shrank and shrank until she disappeared, but I like to imagine her petting animals as she walks in a straight line, up and down a hall.

THE FIRST POET TO FUCK ON THE MOON WILL OFFICIALLY WIN POETRY

My MFA thesis is the rugburn on my knees as I pray to my Otterbox while seventeen Midwestern ghosts sway in the breeze. I defend my thesis by dueling with a Pulitzer Prize. We both lose.

UNTITLED

I wear socks to bed and still stay your favorite fuck.

I WROTE THIS POEM WHILE LISTENING TO BELLE AND SEBASTIAN'S "IT COULD HAVE BEEN A BRILLIANT CAREER"

Someone stuffed my pillows with goodbyes, and now I have to break my heart in multiples of hummingbird. I felt dumber yesterday. For foreplay, we play connect the em dashes. We buy a bigger water heater so we can have shower sex and finish without turning arctic. Last night I dreamt Morrissey falling out of a tree, Rivers Cuomo leaving Weezer to join the Rentals, the Strokes pretending to break up so they'd have a reason to go on a reunion tour, and then I'm awake, dressed in the robe we stole from the Hyatt in Nashville, coughing an ice storm. You're next to me in bed. I push my face into the small of your back and tell you, *There's never enough pancakes in pancakes.* I tell you, *I miss Milwaukee even though I've never been.* You tell me you bought a plot of crater-front property on the moon. *An investment,* you say. *Something to leave our future grandchildren.* For our seventh anniversary, we fuck on a cloud. I decide to go back to college and get a degree in teaching yetis how to hide. I write my term paper on never having to leave a bar alone. My professor gives me an A in jaywalking.

POEM WRITTEN WITH THE SOLE PURPOSE OF TRYING TO MAKE YOU NOSTALGIC ABOUT MY LAST POETRY COLLECTION, *YOUR FAVORITE POET*, ALSO PUBLISHED BY MALARKEY BOOKS, WHICH IS A BETTER BOOK THAN THIS ONE, THE ONE THAT YOU'RE CURRENTLY READING, SO IF YOU HAVEN'T PURCHASED A COPY OF YOUR FAVORITE POET YET, WHICH WAS ALSO PUBLISHED BY MALARKEY BOOKS, THEN YOU SHOULD DEFINITELY BUY IT NOW, LIKE RIGHT THIS SECOND, LIKE STOP READING THIS STUPIDLY LONG TITLE FOR A POEM AND GO BUY IT, AND IF YOU'RE WONDERING WHERE YOU CAN FIND A COPY OF YOUR FAVORITE POET, PUBLISHED BY MALARKEY BOOKS, YOU CAN GET IT DIRECTLY FROM THE PUBLISHER'S WEBSITE OR THROUGH AMAZON.COM OR BOOKSHOP.ORG OR IN PERSON AT POWELL'S, WHICH IS LOCATED IN PORTLAND, OREGON, NOT PORTLAND, MAINE, IN CASE YOU WERE CONFUSED, OR IF IT'S STILL IN STOCK, YOU CAN WALK INTO RAVEN BOOK STORE, WHICH IS LOCATED IN LAWRENCE, KANSAS, AND PICK UP A COPY, BUT ANYWAY, NOW YOU KNOW THERE ARE A LOT OF PLACES YOU CAN BUY YOUR FAVORITE POET, WHICH WAS PUBLISHED BY MALARKEY BOOKS, A BOOK THAT IS BETTER THAN THIS ONE

Over a cup of black coffee and a buttered piece of burned toast, I ask Siri how many people are bleeding right now, in this moment, not this moment now, but that moment, the first moment in this sentence when I first asked Siri about people and blood and numbers, but Siri doesn't say anything because Siri doesn't know—Siri can't even guess—and then it's the afternoon and I'm looking through the living room window, staring at my neighbor's lawn, which is lost in drought and mostly brown—the type of color I imagine snapping under my feet—and my neighbor's lawn just sits there staring back, and I want to ask my neighbor's lawn if it knows it's dying, but I'm too worried about the walls around me, which are shedding their paint, chip by chip, a malaise, the drip of an IV, and there's a baby crying in the other room and I don't know how the baby got there, and no one is around to ask but Siri, but I can't ask Siri because Siri doesn't know—no one does.

POEM ABOUT FRIDAY NIGHT LIGHTS, KYRIE IRVING, AND AARON RODGERS THAT ALSO REFERENCES THE FLAMING LIPS

Tyra Collette doesn't remember laughter, but she once walked on ice that used to be water. Dillon is someone's name and a town in Texas and a panther, and they play football there sometimes, in Dillon, the town in Texas—always on Fridays, in a stadium the size of the coliseum, where there is the same amount of blood left on the field as on the wooden floor covered in Roman sand. QB1 is Texas's favorite sexual position. Jason Street's memory of legs is based on a true story. In Dillon, they play football sometimes. I already mentioned that. Always on Fridays. I already mentioned that, too. Today is one of those Fridays: Matt Saracen scrambling out of the pocket before throwing the football to Tim Riggins, and it's Tim Riggins, gripping the skinned pig, who begins running toward the endzone, and it's Tim Riggins who keeps running past the endzone, running and running and running so far he ends up in the future, in a memory of where—in the Midwest stuffed with cheese—Aaron Rodgers takes a bath in borax and calls Kyrie Irving to see if he'll be at the next flat earth meeting, since Kyrie missed the last one after accidentally locking himself in a closet in James Harden's beard, but Kyrie Irving can't come to the phone right now because he tripped and fell off the side of the earth, and he is either flying or falling, it's hard to tell, but it doesn't matter which because, regardless, breath is hard to find, and as Kyrie Irving flies or falls or something in the middle, he thinks about season two of *Friday Night Lights* and how it got a bit off track with the murder subplot, where the ugly Matt Damon, who doesn't use tissues or his sleeve, pushes a dead body over the bridge and into the river, and how even so, rocky subplot and all, it was still a solid season.

AN EXCERPT FROM TAYLOR SWIFT'S DIARY ENTRY WRITTEN SEVEN MONTHS AFTER BREAKING UP WITH TAYLOR LAUTNER

One time I fucked a guy with the same name as mine because I wanted a reason to scream my own name when I came.

AN ESSAY ABOUT TIME TRAVEL

I remember the lake. I remember the fire. I remember the house. I remember the lake across the street from the house. I remember the fire in the house across the street from the lake. I remember spring in gloom, fireflies dressed as ash or vice versa—ash dressed like the nature of summer. I never know the feeling of what it is to forget to remember, and so I remember the lake. The fire. The house. Wood snapping from the chin, and sirens—one siren is too many, eight sirens is a herd—and I was outside, I remember, I was the girl outside, down by the lake, across the street from the house that swallowed who we will never forget.

THE ONE WHERE ERIC AND DYLAN WALK INTO A LIBRARY

It's spring—April, to be exact—and in fourteen days minus twenty-three years, Eric Harris and Dylan Klebold will walk into a school for the last time. Soon after walking into the school, ten hearts in a library will learn how to stop beating. Twenty-three years later minus fourteen days, the mockingbirds are back. They're trying to nest in my parents' patio—the same place they nested the year before—but my parents screened in their patio and now the mockingbirds are confused. The mockingbirds yell and throw their beaks in the air, stabbing the sky. They fly in circles before landing on the gutter next to my parents' patio and look at the last place they knew where to start, unsure of where tomorrow will go.

MONSTER MONSTER MONSTER

You find a monster hiding under your bed.

The monster is sick. It tells you so. The monster says it has a broken pulse.

You feel bad for the sick monster, so you give it antihistamines, expensive tissues coated with aloe. You check the monster's forehead. The monster is running a fever. You run it a cool bath. In the bath, the monster whittles a bar of soap into a half moon. After the half moon, the monster keeps whittling and whittling until the soap is a crescent moon, until it is zero moons.

You realize no one has ever told the monster when to quit.

You are happy the monster is here. You have been lonely for so long: Years before the boy who never owned a pair of pajamas left; years before you found the bar with the menu of mistakes; years before your father forgot to exist. Years before your daughter decided to almost come but then at the last minute, gave up and quit. Years before you were given pills to cure parts of you you never knew existed.

Too long, your therapist always tells you. *You always wait too long*.

What your therapist doesn't realize, you want to tell him, is that any length of loneliness is too long. The monster is sick sick sick, but, well, shit, anywhere that is anywhere is sick sick sick. Secretly, you hope the monster stays sick. You enjoy taking care of something that isn't yourself. You tried the gardening thing, but your thumb is more highlighter than green, so even the weeds gave up and died. The chrysanthemums never had a chance. And yet, you were surprised when James packed up his Subaru and backed out of the driveway, drove down the block and through the middle of town and into the next county, then past the state line and the state line past that state line.

The monster asks for cucumber water, but you don't have any cucumbers.

You tell the monster you could run out for some cucumbers. Really, it's no big deal—nothing more than a key in the ignition, a quick drive to Kroger. You are so eager to please, to have a reason to buy cucumbers, to take yoga lessons and eat kale, to lie in bed at night staring at your phone, swiping *right right right*. But the monster doesn't say anything. It just stares at its monster hands, so you go into the kitchen and make a pot of chamomile tea.

While waiting for the tea to boil, you wonder what type of person has cucumbers lying around their house, and if you would ever be that type of person. Maybe you will fall in love with that type of person, this cucumber man. You imagine the cucumber man's hands the size of redwoods. You imagine him the longest living organism on Earth.

The monster is no longer staring at its hands. The monster is over the disappointment of not having cucumber water.

You find yourself jealous of how quickly the monster gets over disappointment. When you get down you stay there, so close to the dirt it seeps inside your lungs.

The monster asks for a beer.

Beer, you have. You even have pint glasses in the freezer, frosted, ready for the cucumber man or a sick monster hiding under your bed. You pour the monster a glass of beer. It fizzes inside the frosted mug. The monster takes a sip of the beer. The monster says the beer tastes like sand. The monster says the beer tastes like a cloud following a landslide.

Who is to say no? How could you ever know the taste buds of a monster's tongue?

The monster tells you how it once read an article about the germs that accumulate on cellphones, how the phones can be dirtier than a public toilet, so the monster makes sure to clean its iPhone every night with a Clorox wipe. The monster is so careful it can't understand how it could be so sick. The monster says it remembers when simple addition meant something. The monster says it remembers when a headache only came the morning after a night of too much gin swirling in tonic. You didn't know monsters got hangovers, but you also didn't know that monsters existed or that beer and sand taste the same to a monster.

The monster wonders how the bad follows it. You wonder the same thing about yourself. The monster says this could never be a question, that stating a fact would be a dumb question. You agree, you tell the monster.

The monster wants to know is everywhere sin or is this just breath? And did God make the iceberg or did the iceberg make God?

You tell the monster the truth, which is you don't know. You tell the monster what you do know, that terrible isn't just hiding behind every corner. Terrible is every corner.

Day falls into night. The monster climbs back under your bed. The monster's eyes are soggy. You ask the monster if it wants you to read it a book. You still have the children's books on the shelf—*The Magic School Bus, Curious George, The Giving Tree, Love You Forever*—their spines still solid, unopened since you picked them up at the Books-A-Million off Kingston, before it went out of business and was turned into a Gold's Gym.

You wonder if you will ever read anyone to sleep.

The monster doesn't answer. The monster is already asleep, lost in fever dreams. You imagine what those dreams could possibly be. Maybe the monster walking into a wall. Maybe the monster walking through a wall. Maybe the monster walking toward the sun until the monster is burning, until the monster is ash.

You think about your own dreams. Your therapist said to keep a dream journal on your nightstand. *What's the harm?* he said. You imagine the monster dreaming faces on the backs of milk cartons, watching Elvis twist on a balcony in Venice, a door welded home.

A LIST OF SYNONYMS FOR THE WORD *GHOST*

Sweat-stained hips. A guitar strap on an album cover. Eating your twin in utero. A broken condom caught in a sewer grate. Six fried Mississippis followed by a laugh track. Body aches in the throat. Threats of failing economics. A bar tab wondering, *You okay there, bud?* Warm milk. Tummy tucks just off the interstate. A bereavement card that reads, *Hey, Mom, it's been a while.* T9 on a Blackberry. A Taking Back Sunday reunion tour. Thinking about changing the battery in the smoke alarm but winning the lottery instead. Jellyfish coastlines. A mother, angry, her voice Soundcloud as she says, *Go to your room.* Bullet in the chin, bullet in the neck, bullet in the hip. Bumper stickers in the Florida panhandle. Nuking a hurricane. The last swig of Listerine. Hair tied around a wrist. Hair tied around other hair. Bedsheets left in the dryer. An eighteen-car pileup. Adderall + Xanax + IPA. The chicken sandwich wars. A bullet in the brain. HAHAHAHAHAHAHAHA. Sometimes we call it *poetry*. Icarus's headache right before.

A LIST OF WHAT I FOUND IN THE RESTROOM OF THE TACO BELL OFF KINGSTON BOULEVARD

Julia Roberts's smile. A cave drawing of a cave. A rollercoaster shaped like a cross. Pete Davidson's face tattooed on your ex's cock. An umbrella left at a restaurant, shoved in the Lost & Found bin. Fabric softener. Cracked ribs under a beige turtleneck. A faucet going *drip drip drip*. A missile covered in toes. Gerard Butler drinking a fourth mojito on a set in Toronto that's supposed to look like California. A dented Magic 8 Ball excavated in the Badlands. Logistical nightmare. A man, burnt from the knees up, whispering, *What happened to all the leftover patio furniture?* A lover's heart on airplane mode. Pillow talk. The cashier at Whole Foods flirting with the wind. The first fever. A wolf flossing its molars with a red cape. Ex-boyfriend #3 moonlighting as ex-boyfriend #5. Breath locked in a submarine. Frankly, the ocean. Midnight Mass. The Pepsi Challenge. *I choose violence*, written on the bathroom stall with the middle of a chalupa. *No, I said nothing*. And yet. *When you go, miss me twice.*

MY DAUGHTER KEEPS DROPPING FOOD ON THE FLOOR AND NOW THE DOG IS BECOMING OBESE

Purgatory is nothing but a commercial break, followed by an infomercial, a waiting room—fluorescent, flickering, the scene before the credits roll, a dream painted on a beige wall. Motel art. How long does it take for a heart to decompose? If medicine tasted like Skittles, then every rainbow would be dripping citrus or scented zombie or falling asleep on a park bench or a bloated skyline across the Atlantic. Fifteen shots. Four dead. Six halfway there. There is so much I don't know, like why in a library in 1999, it only took two hearts to make ten hearts stop beating. Or why people buy plastic fruit. Or why my daughter has to live here and breathe here and love here and pet a dog here and to and fro here and here and here, and I don't know what to say because there is nothing to say when people buy guns the size of legs while I dream my teeth rotten as my molars climb right out of me.

I THOUGHT ABOUT THE FILM *GOOD WILL HUNTING*—DIRECTED BY OSCAR-NOMINEE GUS VAN SANT (*DRUGSTORE COWBOY, MILK, ELEPHANT*), AND STARRING OSCAR-WINNER MATT DAMON (*THE BOURNE IDENTITY, THE BOURNE SUPREMACY, WE BOUGHT A ZOO*) AS MATH PRODIGY WILL HUNTING, AND OSCAR-WINNER BEN AFFLECK (*GIGLI, MALLRATS, REINDEER GAMES*) AS MATH PRODIGY WILL HUNTING'S BEST FRIEND, AND OSCAR-NOMINEE MINNIE DRIVER (*RETURN TO ME, RETURN TO ZERO, HOPE SPRINGS*) AS MATH PRODIGY WILL HUNTING'S LOVE INTEREST, AND OSCAR-WINNER ROBIN WILLIAMS (*DEAD POETS SOCIETY, MRS. DOUBTFIRE, JUMANJI*) AS MATH PRODIGY WILL HUNTING'S PSYCHOLOGIST WHO HAS A PENCHANT FOR BEARDS AND BOOKS AND CAN'T GET OVER THE WAY HIS DEAD WIFE USED TO FART IN HER SLEEP—APPROXIMATELY FOUR TIMES WHILE WRITING THIS POEM

It is illegal to put lead in paint, but you can stuff it in flesh. Even awake I worry my teeth are growing arms, pressing saws to gums. *Who will be buried next?* I ask my doctor's doctor. I ask the priest who's putting pieces of Jesus into people's mouths, *Do you need a blue or black ink pen to sign up for the waitlist to heaven?* I ask the barista at Starbucks, *What happens to the rest of us when a bullet makes your heart go blank?* The barista shrugs, though he puts an extra shot in my latte. Lately, everywhere I look it's nothing but shoulders pressed against other shoulders. It's kids climbing over other kids, screaming in caps lock. It's an unanswered math problem written on a chalkboard that asks, *If a train leaves Boulder at 2 p.m. and it's going seventy miles per hour, while at the same time someone coughs blood in Cedar Bluff, how do you lock a door that's already locked?*

I TAKE A ROCKET INTO SPACE AND FORGET WHY I WENT INTO SPACE

The Weather Channel states that by the afternoon there will be a forty-two percent chance of flesh and bone and teeth wrapped in skin. It's morning. The alarm clock flashes *first cup of coffee*. I pour snowflakes over my bowl of Lucky Charms as I check Zillow for new listings in the town I built inside a snow globe. I find an all-brick rancher off Main Street, so I go to the credit union I built between the bodega that sells poets to the birds and the vending machine that sells smaller vending machines outside the split-level tattoo/coffee shop. I tell the banker at the credit union that I built a home for my home, and that I need a loan for the home I built for my home. The banker runs my credit score and frowns. I tell the banker, *It's okay, I sold five more copies of my chapbook about dating Pete Davidson just last week.* I tell the banker that my daughter is ambivalent toward the weather, but that one day she will learn how to swim. The banker doesn't say anything. I tell the banker my bank account is now an accordion. The banker still doesn't say anything. The banker has a face, and that face is enough.

A COMPREHENSIVE LIST OF PLACES TO HIDE FROM A BULLET

SETLIST FOR LEIGH CHADWICK'S NORTH AMERICAN TOUR

HOW DO I TELL MY DAUGHTER WHEN SHE IS OLD ENOUGH FOR ME TO TELL HER

that drills don't just build houses, that sometimes a broken window is nothing more than a broken window, that numbers grow like weeds, that the air gets thick when candles burn at dusk while parents are swabbed for DNA, that it's best to close your eyes, that sometimes a body is too soft to stay a body, that I'm sorry my legs will never be fast enough?

HOW MANY TIMES IS TOO MANY TIMES TO LISTEN TO REGINA SPEKTOR'S "US" ON REPEAT?

Dressed in matching cardigans, sharing a pair of AirPods, sitting on a park bench on a September afternoon.

Or:

You, promising never to dog-ear my heart.

Or:

A half-open bedroom door, the walls the color of a famous actress's teeth, a mattress on the floor. My lips pressed against your shoulder blade as I tell you, *I like it here*, and you say, *Well, then, maybe you should just stay.*

I WAS STILL LISTENING TO BELLE AND SEBASTIAN'S "IT COULD HAVE BEEN A BRILLIANT CAREER" WHEN I WROTE THIS POEM

I was never given an origin story, but my left leg failed high school gym class twice. My chest aches whenever I cough thunder. My misery walks into a wall while my depression buys a lottery ticket. My ticket matches three out of the five numbers, and I win an extra side effect from my Lexapro. It's winter, but I'm crawling through spring. The Ouija board says we are older than we were yesterday. I tell the cashier at Whole Foods, *I swear I'd be famous if I hadn't lost my retainer in the seventh grade.* I stopped smoking when I started flirting with mothers. Still, your eyes have stayed the color of a lighter that went through the wash but still works. We have a daughter and name her after a song that smells like jasmine. I keep our youth wrapped in cellophane, hidden in the back of the fridge. We decide to buy a house so our daughter can have somewhere to grow up to resent us. I always slam the bedroom door so we have a reason to go to couple's therapy, where I dab my eyes with a tissue and tell the therapist that what I miss the most is my elbows pressed against the balcony in Courtney Square, your lips a preheated oven against my collarbone, as I counted down the eight minutes it took to smoke my first post-dawn, pre-fuck cigarette of the day.

I CALL YOU MY HUSBAND

You are asleep in my bed. I watch your chest rise and fall while outside, thunder announces that there will be a tomorrow. As I watch you, I wonder if you will always be good at being my husband. I wonder if sex will always feel like a third margarita at 2:37 p.m. on a Saturday in May. I wonder if anything can be a question if you call it a question. I wonder if an octopus lost one of its hearts, would it be happier?

I WANT TO LIVE SOFTLY

I get a job selling jobs to people who need jobs. I build amusement parks in the veins of lovers, attach harps to the lungs of the song about balloons. I burn the sun, glue Tylenol to the achy bridge that is always crawling over Clinch River. I rhyme the word *orange* with *orange*. I take lessons on forgetting how to dance. I tattoo *I'd wear you home if only you'd fit* on the kneecap of the last elephant.

EVERY DAY IS A GOOD DAY TO LISTEN TO "SOMEDAY" (REMASTERED)

Every day is the most common day to get shot in the neck. To smell wild. To plant tulips in your tea. Every night, I put on my dancing shoes before climbing into bed. It doesn't take much to understand the brilliance of sorrow. It's not *if* I see but *when*. Anything can be a sin if you have to change your clothes after. Since the early aughts, I've been hiding my memories in the trunk of my car: The night we drank the lake. The night that ended with us blowing into empty champagne flutes. The morning of flutter that followed. Crying into cardigans I've hidden from moths. The moss covering the poem where you walked down the middle of the street, blindfolded, your stomach filled with swirls of blue. The poem you left between my thighs. The poem pressed against my gums. Springsteen's ass as cover art. Spilled aspartame on the kitchen counter. The shower head against my skin. Your cock. The shed of leftover lumber from the half-built birdhouses, long abandoned, full of rot. The broken medicine cabinet. Nothing from 2020. The night you sang the beach to sea. Surely, you know. The second broken medicine cabinet. That time in the garage with the lightning pressed mute. Always, the rain. The dog bed that lost its smell. An empty picture frame. The cobwebs in the attic. The sheets bleached ghost. The smell of the hospital room. The supermoon that looked the same as every other moon. The first time our daughter reached and reached and kept reaching until her fingers found my chin.

IT'S TRUE

In the beginning, no one knew it was the beginning.

AN EMPTY CLOSET IS STILL A CLOSET

I dress in the Cold War. I dress in Xanax. I dress in hiccups and prayers, report cards, fuccbois, and broken colored pencils. I dress Alexa in folded tongue. I dress going the wrong way. I dress Phoebe Bridgers in more Phoebe Bridgers. I dress New York in soil and grow the last fruit eaten in Eden. I dress in Bon Iver's cabin. I dress yesterday's weather in a ribbon and bow and toss it in the green dumpster behind Starbucks. I dress the U-turn I always miss on Johnson Street. I dress tomorrow in your sweaty monologue about the river running north.

UNCORRECTED PROOF

This was when you were living in a studio apartment just a leg outside of Nashville. You were messing around with J. who called himself a *Brony*, though you didn't know what that meant and were always too afraid to ask. These were the years when you were mostly alone, spending your days in bed, a lit American Spirit in your left hand, an ashtray asleep on your stomach. The walls of the studio apartment were paper thin, so whenever the two of you fucked, J. would try to hide your moans by pressing his mouth against yours while his hands grabbed your ass, lifting you up as he pushed himself further inside you. This is how you knew he was getting close. This was also how you knew you were not going to get close. You rented the studio apartment just a leg outside of Nashville for two years. During that time, you worked nights at a bar that pretended to be a restaurant and spent your days practicing how to live. Eventually, J. stopped coming by, and as the mornings waned into early afternoons, you kept looking out the one window in the apartment, which faced the parking lot, and absently gazed at the cars pulling in and out of the parking spaces as you popped Xanax like cough drops. Then, a month before you quit the bar that pretended to be a restaurant, you met a man who smelled like a husband, all redwood and mismatched socks. You felt how a heart could beat comely. You ran out of Xanax and barely cared. You taught yourself how to build a religion inside a Moleskine. Then the man who smelled like a husband became a man who you called *husband*, followed by the house in the suburbs, getting pregnant and then forgetting how to be pregnant, throwing all of your silverware into the trash, getting pregnant again and then forgetting how to be pregnant, again, until, finally, you learned how to stop forgetting.

ANYTHING CAN HAPPEN IN A PARK IF YOU CALL EVERYTHING A PARK

I walk in a straight line. I learn how to never drown. I taste everything twice. I gain ten pounds from dreaming in French. I make out with the history of the woods. I dance more than I did yesterday. I laugh in tandem. I wonder, *Goddamn, when did the sky grow so eternal?* I grow a synthesizer in your chest and imagine fucking someone who has the same name as you.

I WANTED TO NAME MY DAUGHTER PRIMROSE
BUT EVERYONE SAID NO, LEIGH, THAT'S DUMB,
SO I DIDN'T NAME MY DAUGHTER PRIMROSE,
BUT NO ONE CAN TELL ME WHAT I CAN OR
CAN'T TITLE MY POEMS, SO FUCK IT, THIS
POEM IS TITLED "PRIMROSE"

I never have a reason to talk about parsley. Remember June. The bugs. The bugs eating other bugs. Dusk. The dress made of sun hiked above my waist. The house on Clinch Street. Writing fanfiction about myself while you bathed in adjectives. Afternoons spent fucking on the back of a humpback whale even though we never went near the ocean. And that time you woke me up with the hum of tender tides after I built you a chest of armor and called you *space travel*, followed by fifteen sounds that were later stolen after being left in a deserted parking lot.

DELETED SCENES FROM THE MUSIC VIDEO FOR CAKE'S 2001 HIT SONG "SHORT SKIRT / LONG JACKET"

I find the word *foliage* sexy, so I take you into the woods behind the smaller woods, where I spend the dew-soaked early hours covering myself in your bark. Nine months later, I birth an apple tree. We name the apple tree Eve. I plant Eve in the backyard. You build a fence around her. After, you put a sign on the fence: *PRIVATE PROPERTY: NO ADAMS ALLOWED*. I spend my days in the backyard, killing every weed that looks at her sideways. I teach Eve arithmetic, animal husbandry, small engine repair, and how to properly phrase prepositions. I tell her the difference between love and touching the wrist of a cornfield and writing ghost stories set in Maine and using your tongue to tie the stem of a cherry into a knot. Sitting under Eve, we sing shadows at dusk. We hold hands as we watch our daughter grow and grow, until she is towering over us, and we can no longer count the hours we spend together in shade.

MVP

I vote your index finger the MVP of my third-favorite orgasm.

WHILE ON THE VERGE OF WANTING TO JUMP OFF A CLIFF, I WRITE A POEM

I am tired of being scared of being scared. I am tired of being. I am tired of billionaires not exploding in the sky. I am tired of never having a reason to say the word *marsupial*. I am tired of wondering how many people died today and why and if body bags ever commit suicide. I am tired of never having a reason to buy a guitar, so I decide to start a cover band that covers cover bands. I am tired of never washing my hair under a waterfall. I am tired of never screaming, *Give me Mario Kart or give me Mario Kart* while getting fucked in the breakroom of a GameStop. I am tired of waiting for a poem to finish itself. I am tired of how we lose everything and if we didn't lose it then it was never ours to begin with.

WHAT COMMAS

Kill the commas, Adrienne sends through email, though the words are in all caps. *KILL THE COMMAS*. We are working with our editor on the final edits for our collection, *Too Much Tongue*. And so we kill the commas, hit the *Backspace* and then *Ctrl + S*, and now they're gone, the commas, like they never existed in the first place, and this act of deletion makes me think of space gas, though I don't know why, and then I'm thinking about dinosaurs and I know exactly why, and then I'm looking down the hall and there's my daughter asleep in her crib, which will soon need to be a bed because everything changes, leaves, just quits being what we thought it would always be, and as I archive the email, I know that by the time I go to sleep tonight, I will have forgotten why the commas were spoken of in the first place.

NOVEMBER IS A MONTH I GUESS

I can't understand how an entire state can vote the color of blood while another state floods from an ocean, any ocean, and how up and down the west coast, sprinklers are never built in forests, and how everything isn't screaming or growling or trying to medicine the sky, or what it means to still the birdsong of my hummingbird's heart or watch hope drain from the Mississippi, but who cares when everything lost or gone or both floats like thought bubbles above our heads and through the air, all air, the thought bubbles that can't keep the weeks in place, the months that follow the promise of a year or two in wrinkles.

DUETS

WHAT COMES NEXT
Co-written with Adrienne Marie Barrios

I listen to *The Sunlandic Twins* while scrubbing my bathroom with starfish. Last night, I ate spaghetti. It tasted like spaghetti. Lately I've found myself laughing in slow motion. It's a thing, I suppose. Just another thing. At the same moment, you wake up before the alarm you never set. You stretch like a cough and yawn a laugh track. Out of bed, and then you're in the bathroom. Standing in front of the bathroom mirror, you watch your head swell until it is a balloon. Then you're floating inches off the ground as you brush your teeth in the most boring way. After running out of starfish to scrub my bathroom with, I spend the rest of the day capitalizing my orgasms. I wonder why I've never owned a pair of overalls or why I've never met a comet or never read *Goodnight, Moon* to a tired rainforest after tucking it into bed. You spit the toothpaste out of your mouth. You try to count to ten but forget how, though you have no idea why you began counting to ten in the first place. You give up counting. Your head is still a balloon. You're still floating as you think, *Helium begets helium begets helium.* You are inches above the ground then feet and then you are scraping the ceiling. You crane your neck and stare at the ceiling and wonder if anyone has ever cleaned a ceiling and if so, how many starfish did it take?

THERE IS NO ANSWER TO THE SIMPLICITY OF WEATHER
Co-written with Mitchell Nobis

My dreams are nothing but a wall of owls. I wake up all eyes and twisted thumbs. The birds are back in predawn spring. I'm stuck in an alarm clock of sweetness and tweets as the river pushes heavy with dead winter and trash. Benches are free unless you're poor. I think about church, but I don't know why. I cross my mouth. I consider thinking about Memphis. I used to love, and I still do. I imagine swallowing grime under my fingernails. I imagine a medicine cabinet full of nail clippings. I imagine my sweat dripping into the river, pushing the dying and dead trash south. Would it get there by winter? Would I? I blink back the urge to dive headfirst down the stairs like a shortstop catching a shot. I want a reason to crossover into a finger roll. I look up. I feel close enough to the sky to be trapped in a postcard. Eagles circle overhead. They want to eat my liver, regenerating downriver forever. I always remember. I tell them so. I never trust them.

WHAT SWALLOWS BUT DOESN'T SEE
Co-written with Mitchell Nobis

A sundress lumped in dust and asphalt, alone in the middle of Grand River Avenue. I am filled with questions for the questions about the questions I have yet to question. Like, who undressed the first sundress, and what happens when a naked body washes ashore and there's no one there to yell, *Cut!* and is the sundress—all cotton flowers once yellow, now dusted brown—hours or days or years later, still alone in the middle of the avenue missed, missing while being missed? Jump cut, wipe, fade, or dissolve. Who leaves the sun in the middle of a poem, and where does the body of a dress go when it just slips out of the fabric, and what is there left to do but yell, *Cut!* and turn the camera off, count to five thousand sheep, dream rivers deep, get buffeted by currents and eddies only to wake up to a summer in June, the morning's drunk hunger reaching greens to the thousand-soul clouds leaving the dress as it melts against the pavement? Do we melt, boil, or burn? A tire is a tire regardless of where it goes. A truck is hungry wherever it turns, rumbles as it swallows what it doesn't see: the body of what kept the dress, the present tense of past. Where is the camera? A blue sign with a white *H*. The cold of a basement. Someone missing a dress. Someone missing.

I LIKE TO THINK PROPER FIRST THING IN THE MORNING
Co-written with Andrew Bertaina

I should like to write a poem about sex, but I'm nervous about learning how to walk through walls. I've been thinking a lot about thinking of late, reading everyone who has also been preoccupied with thought: Aristotle, Wittgenstein, the collection of parents on my local Facebook group, the 2006 Sears Catalog, my sister who wrote me a letter informing me she's happy to be my sister. We're thinking together, making a massive sort of project of thinking, like Noah and his Ark. Is Michael Jordan still crying? GIF should be spelled with a *J*, that's some bullshit. My daughter asks why we stuck Earth in a toaster. I don't know what to say—my brain is full of elephants—so I tell her, *It's so easy to dream in regret when you make it to last call.* I'm sorry. I know this poem was supposed to be about sex, but I keep tripping down the stairs, like the summer my two best friends kept inviting me over to hang out with two cute girls, but I always said no, instead spending the afternoons tucked inside a role-playing-game called Dark Wizard. *What happened to that boy?* someone asks. He grew up afraid to write poems about sex.

PLEASE MIX AND MESH AND MOLD AND FOLD
Co-written with Ben Niespodziany

Despite the woodland science, everyone is dead or dying. 2028 is already gone. Still, I pray to the cicada obeying my breast. The rug-burned make-up sex. Throw pillows on the floor. I mispronounce breath. I mispronounce grace. I break my arm falling on an em dash. I cry smoke signals. I soak my eyes in a jug of wine. Outside, the forest is drunk. In bed, naked, is where you are my favorite. It's exhausting constantly carrying around a bag of wings. Outside is the mirage of God walking backwards. Still the valley is the same. I'm trying to fix a fan on my own. Everything billows.

DAY TO DAY
Co-written with Mitchell Nobis

Dark morning, red blinking lights—stopped behind the school bus three stories high and shaped like a mushroom—I think *tentacles*. Waiting for the children to stop being children, I try to think about solving something, anything—to find a way to better what will never be better: mass shootings followed by *thoughts and prayers*, a tepid Arctic, our poison air. Instead, it's the ninety-two mistakes I made yesterday or how Kawhi Leonard could come back home from Toronto with knees made of glass and tin toys. I try again to think more important thoughts: hallways of middle schools and supermarkets and warehouses bleeding, the difference between *thoughts and prayers* and *over my dead body*, the number of emotions it takes to get to infinity, and how easy it is to hyperventilate when you don't want to hyperventilate. I try to breathe through my mouth, but my lungs are clogged. I try to slow down but my heart turns punching bag. I am cracked. I am chemically imbalanced. I am retribution. I am least likely to dot dot dot. When did my brain become a distorted amp? I am lost in feedback. *Put me on the injured reserve*, I'd tell my coach if I had a coach. *I'm day to day.*

HOSPITAL GOWN
Co-written with Ben Niespodziany

I glutton my mourns. I bury my caskets in upside down attics. An atlas of cigarette burns. I take my gunpowder with coffee and cream. I brave lengthy afternoons without a helmet or cross. It was a decade and a month ago when I lost the left side of my heart in a freak kissing accident. I don't like to talk about it. Saccharine in a white lab coat, I tell the doctor, *On a scale of one to ten, I am a two*. My metal within is wallet-sized. It clamps to my heart like a starter kit. How it wishes to pump like new.

THAT'S STILL SHORT TERM.
I CARE ABOUT LONG TERM.
Co-written with Adrienne Marie Barrios

You spend your afternoon chipping commas and drinking tea that goes cold the minute it's born. You say, *I care little about what's said in the short term.* You crack your shoulder blades. You wonder if you water them, would they grow wings? You say, *I care about what happens tomorrow or the next day or the end of next month when the doctor pronounces my heart obsolete.* You imagine me standing in my kitchen, drinking a margarita. You ask, *What will we do when the trees stop growing fruit?* I answer, *We'll mix tequila with tequila and forget that anything ever existed.* We both nod. You imagine white feathers sprouting from your shoulder blades, grazing your neck. You smile. That seems right.

HIT SINGLES

GREG ABBOTT CAN GO FUCK HIMSELF

It was not the girl's blood, but she took it, smeared it all over her cheeks, the same cheeks her mother kissed before she walked down the street to get on the school bus, and as I sit on my couch and watch the news, I can't stop wondering what her mother fed her for breakfast that morning, before she borrowed her friend's blood, before the DNA swabs and the cookie jars filled with thoughts and prayers, and as I continue to watch the news, I can't stop wondering when a number stops being a number, or when fog grows weeds. I'd ask my therapist, but I don't have a therapist. Is that something I should admit? I am sad in a sad way. I haven't felt the same since I imagined Sandy walking around with a hook for a hand. Still, yesterday my daughter said the word *bubbles*. Still, I've never shot a gun, but this morning I fed my daughter waffles—her mouth full as she hummed the word *yum* in reverse. Right now, she has her thumb in her mouth, her stuffed rabbit clutched against her chest, as she watches an episode of *Sesame Street*. What the politicians on the news keep saying is that two doors is too many, and that locks don't have to be broken to not work. By the time the episode of *Sesame Street* ends, my daughter has dropped her stuffed rabbit and is reaching for her wand of bubbles. Soon, I will take her outside, spin the wand full of soapy water around as she chases the bubbles, trying to catch what was never meant to stay.

APRIL IS ITS OWN WEATHER

I spend the night dreaming dumb and the morning waking up zombie, painted in nothing, coughing fireflies. My emotions have a head cold, and the iPhone caught inside my temporal lobe won't stop going *buzz buzz buzz*. I'm feeling dangerous, so I go bowling without socks, pour wine into more wine, say *yes* to every question that ends with *yes?* April is the best month to call April. Every spring, I fall in love with [redacted] and birth a [redacted]. My favorite afternoons are the ones spent hunched over a barstool, wearing a head full of bees, consumed by thoughts of walking across my lawn dressed as fingertips filled with gloam.

IF THE TRUTH IS OUT THERE, I QUIT

There is a season where Oklahoma does nothing but swirl. In Maine, mud chews the days between winter and spring. Someone needs to give Mississippi some water; it's dehydrated. For decades, Colorado has been nothing but a season of guns. If you ignore Florida, you'll live longer. Gray chalk blankets Salt Lake City, the Los Angeles skyline, whatever Chattanooga calls Chattanooga. Fossil fuels create more fossils. I could tear the world apart with my teeth. I'm sure something is happening in Montana, but I don't know what. I've never had a reason to ask. Same with Idaho and the worst Dakota. My sister lives in Fargo, but all I know about Fargo is that there's a movie with the same name that takes place in Minnesota and that, even though the instruction manual doesn't state it, woodchippers can be used for more than just wood. In Minnesota, there are two cities that pretend to be one. Everything connects. There's a rumor that someone stole the scarecrows in Iowa, but I haven't checked. One time I watched a bush burn, but it didn't tell me shit. What will my daughter dream about in ten years? I'm too tired to choose my own adventure, so I'm ordering a dream catcher off Amazon. Is Mars red from blushing because it knows we're talking about it? There is no way to end anything without walking into a grocery store and hoping to make it out alive.

ANXIOUS LOVE

You touch my wrist and then wash your hands. You carry our daughter from the kitchen to the living room and then wash your hands. Lately, you've been getting nosebleeds in the shower. When we kiss, I can taste the anxiety on your lips. Your psychiatrist thinks the pills will work this time. Our daughter spits up on your shirt. You change three times before deciding to shower. You say sorry. You are always saying sorry. I make chocolate chip pancakes every Saturday morning. You kiss our daughter on the nose. Her cheeks flush in the sun.

THE GREEN FERN

Sometimes I call it regret and sometimes I call it the flash of wind, the green fern in the waiting room, where I sit and where I wait and where my name is called and where I am told be calm, where I am told to breathe, where I am and where I will always be, where I am told nothing will help but still sit, still be still, still wait, because this is where I will be still in wait when I am eventually placed in a gown and walked to a room as sterile as where I first began.

A POEM NOT ABOUT BEARS

There's beer in the fridge and soap in the bathroom and right now I'm thinking about bears. I don't know why I'm thinking about bears because I don't care about bears. I don't give a fuck about bears. What is there even to say about bears? If I had to write a Yelp review of bears, I would write, *I like that song "Two Weeks" by Grizzly Bear.* And: *That last ten minutes of* Grizzly Man *fucked me up something awful.* But that's about it—two stars at best. I haven't left the house since the last time I left the house. Not because of bears or anything. I just haven't left the house. The last time I left the house, it was a Thursday. I did not think about bears the last time I left the house, which was a Thursday. I did not think about bears on that Thursday, which was the last time I left the house. I did not think about bears once because bears don't matter because I am the sun.

(INTERLUDE)

In the beginning, I'm already here, hidden oceans deep, colored coral and choking seaweed, a melody brought back to life—a rhythm of a chord, a former latchkey child eating Cheetos and reading *Cosmo* as I wait for my parents to come home and tell me to stop eating Cheetos and reading *Cosmo*—and now here I am, again, still in the beginning, still choking seaweed, still waiting and waiting for what you meant when you said, *Stay, just stay,* and so here I am staying, just staying, dressed in whatever you'll promise to keep.

I GOT DEPRESSED SO I DECIDED TO WRITE A BOOK ABOUT BEING DEPRESSED, AND IT'S ACTUALLY THIS BOOK, SOPHOMORE SLUMP, THE ONE YOU'RE HOLDING IN YOUR HANDS (AND GOODNESS, WHAT LOVELY HANDS THEY ARE), THE ONE YOU'VE JUST ABOUT FINISHED READING, AND BY THE WAY, WHILE YOU'RE HERE, LET ME JUST SAY THANK YOU FOR READING IT, THIS LITTLE, SAD BOOK I WROTE AND TITLED SOPHOMORE SLUMP, AND HOPEFULLY YOU BOUGHT THIS COPY YOU'RE READING BECAUSE HOLY SHIT DAYCARE IS EXPENSIVE, BUT EVEN IF YOU DIDN'T BUY IT AND, INSTEAD, YOU SHOPLIFTED IT FROM AN INDEPENDENT BOOKSTORE (PRETTY SHITTY OF YOU, TO BE HONEST) OR READ IT HUNCHED IN THE CORNER OF YOUR LOCAL LIBRARY (THAT WOULD BE OKAY!) OR ORDERED IT OFF AMAZON AND THEN RETURNED IT (STILL PRETTY SHITTY, BUT HEY, WHATEVER) OR STOLE IT FROM AN EX-LOVER (ALSO A TOTALLY OKAY THING TO DO!), I AM STILL GLAD YOU ARE HERE (EMO IN C MINOR)

I'm depressed, so I write a book about being depressed, about being swallowed by a whale and then shooting my way out of the belly of the whale, about fucking you under midnight, about bullet casings in car seats and the first memory of what comes after the afterlife. It's spring. Everything is dying or already dead. Soon, it will be summer, and everything will still be dying or already dead. I hear they've started selling caskets in bulk at Costco. I hear there's a sale on body bags at The Home Depot. I'm told you can find them next to the trash bags, only an aisle or two down from the bulletproof doors and cabinets coated in Kevlar.

THANK YOU

Thank you to my family for being my family. Thank you to Alan for letting me make another book with him. Thank you to Angelo for giving this book such a beautiful cover. Thank you to Adrienne for teaching me about commas and for making these poems look like poems. Thank you to Ben and Adrienne and Mitchell and Andrew for building poems with me and letting me put them in this book. Thank you to the editors who said yes. Thank you to the editors who said no, but please try us again. Thank you to everyone I accidentally forgot to thank. Thank you to Leigh Chadwick. Thank you to (name of Twitter follower) for putting up with my bullshit. Thank you to Jimmy Butler. Thank you to everyone who told me my poems mattered. And thank you, dear reader. Thank you for sharing your time with me. I hope to see you again soon.

ACKNOWLEDGMENTS

Thank you to the editors of the following journals in which some of the poems in this book appeared, often in earlier forms:

Autofocus, Cloves Literary, The Daily Drunk, Eunoia Review, Gone Lawn, Heavy Feather Review, Hobart, Identity Theory, The Leigh Chadwick Review, The Massachusetts Review, Pithead Chapel, Rejection Letters, and *X-R-A-Y Literature.*

"Every Day Is a Good Day to Listen to 'Someday (Remastered)'" originally appeared in *This Is How We learn to Pray*, a poetry coloring book, illustrated by Stephanie Kirsten, published by ELJ Editions in 2021.

ABOUT THE AUTHOR

Leigh Chadwick is the author of *Your Favorite Poet* and the collaborative poetry collection *Too Much Tongue*, co-written with Adrienne Marie Barrios. Her poetry has appeared in *The Massachusetts Review*, *Salamander*, *Passages North*, *The Indianapolis Review*, and *Identity Theory*, among others. She is a regular contributor for *Olney Magazine*, where she conducts the "Mediocre Conversations" interview series.

She can be found online at leighchadwick.com and on Twitter at @LeighChadwick5.

**DELUXE EDITION
WITH BONUS TRACKS**

FOREVER

I find the idea of living forever exhausting, so I decide I will die at the age of eighty-seven. I will begin smoking again at the crisp age of seventy—a week after my husband has his third heart attack and is buried in a plot next to my future plot in the cemetery off Peters Rd. in Oak Ridge. A few months after my husband's death, my daughter, Emily, will divorce her husband after she comes home early from work and finds his hair stylist, Trisha, bent over the living room couch, with her husband—pants and boxers around his ankles—bare-assed behind her. Around this time, I will forget how to feel. I will see a psychiatrist who will prescribe medications that make me forget that I forgot how to feel. After Emily's divorce is finalized, she will move back in with me and spend three years sleeping in her childhood bedroom. I will smoke cigarette after cigarette as I watch my daughter gain twenty-five pounds and then lose forty, as she finds God and then loses him, too. Eventually, Emily will learn how to not lose things, and on a day in a May, she will meet Steve—a chiropractor with twin teenage daughters who always smell like cherry blossoms—in the produce aisle at Kroger. Emily and

Steve will refer to the story of how they met as a meet-cute, though I will have no idea what that means. They will hold hands as they tell me about how they both reached for the same tomato. *The same tomato!* they will say, all teeth and the onset of middle age. *Out of all of the tomatoes in all the Kroger's, we reached for that one!* A year after *the tomato*, Emily and Steve will marry under a tree. It will be a beautiful tree. Emily will never birth a child, and after two miscarriages, Steve will get a vasectomy. The twins will always smell like cherry blossoms. On my seventy-third birthday, I will take on a new lover. His name will be Phil. He will refer to himself as a recovering Baptist. I will suck his cock three times, but he will only come once. We will share a queen bed for six years until Phil passes away in his sleep. *How gentle a ghost crawls through you*, I will think as the paramedics cover Phil with a white sheet and roll him out of the room. After Phil's passing, I will immediately buy a new bed. I will buy cocaine from one of the twins I will never be able to tell apart. I will roll up a twenty-dollar bill and imagine everything a movie. I will only do it once. I will smell cherry blossoms for the entire afternoon. I will like it okay. I will decide to never take another lover, and halfway to eighty-eight, as I step off an escalator in the Midtown Mall, I will fall and break my hip. Three weeks later, I will be dead.

STILL YOUR FAVORITE POET

I've never fucked in the woods—skirt hiked up, back scratched raw from bark—but I've laid on the concrete floor of James's parents' garage and imagined headlights crawling over me. Every third Thursday, I go to therapy, where I tell my therapist, *The last poem I wrote was better.* I've forgotten everything about the afternoon at the lake. On TV, the forecaster says the weekend is filled with whispers of thunderstorms, sleet, tornado watches turning into tornado warnings, snow flurries dressed as yeti sightings. Still, it's a day of making memories, so I take out the trash before masturbating to a picture of you finding the remote control between the couch cushions. Every third Thursday when I go to therapy, I tell my therapist, *If you look hard enough, you can find sex on every letter of the alphabet.* On TV, it's nothing but scattered snow, shoulder blades crumpled in marrow, Fox Mulder cracking sunflowers between his teeth, and a chyron that reads *There is a thirty-eight percent chance you will fall in love four times before it finally sticks.*

OTHER BOOKS PUBLISHED BY MALARKEY BOOKS THAT ARE AVAILABLE DIRECTLY FROM THE PUBLISHER AS WELL AS MOST BOOK RETAILERS INCLUDING AMAZON, BARNES & NOBLE, AND BOOKSHOP IN BOTH PRINT AND EBOOK FORMAT

Faith, a novel by Itoro Bassey
The Life of the Party Is Harder to Find Until You're the Last One Around, poems by Adrian Sobol
Music Is Over, a novel by Ben Arzate
Toadstones, stories by Eric Williams
Deliver Thy Pigs, a novel by Joey Hedger
It Came From the Swamp, an anthology of stories featuring cryptids (aka bigfoot and mermaids and other legendary creatures), edited by Joey Poole
Pontoon, an anthology of fiction and poetry,
Guess What's Different, essays by Susan Triemert
White People on Vacation, a novel by Alex Miller
Your Favorite Poet, poems by Leigh Chadwick, author of *Sophomore Slump*
Man in a Cage, a novel by Patrick Nevins
Fearless, a novel by Benjamin Warner
Don Bronco's (Working Title) Shell, a novel? by Donald Ryan
Un-ruined, a novel by Roger Vaillancourt

Thunder From a Clear Blue Sky, a novel by Justin Bryant
Kill Radio, a novel by Lauren Bolger
Backmask, a novel by OF Cieri
The Muu-Antiques, a novel by Shome Dasgupta
Gloria Patri, a novel by Austin Ross
Where the Pavement Turns to Sand, stories by Sheldon Birnie

Coming in 2024

Still Alive, a novel by LJ Pemberton
Thumbsucker, poems by Kat Giordano
Hope and Wild Panic, stories by Sean Ennis
Sleep Decades, stories by Israel A. Bonilla
I Blame Myself But Also You (and Other Stories), by Spencer Fleury
The Great Atlantic Highway & Other Stories, by Steve Gergley
First Aid for Choking Victims, stories by Matthew Zanoni Müller

malarkeybooks.com

www.ingramcontent.com/pod-product-compliance
Lightning Source LLC
LaVergne TN
LVHW041948070526
838199LV00051BA/2951